Funny Things to Ponder

Steve Vogt

OAC
BOOKS
OSAGE ARTS COMMUNITY

Osage Arts Community Books
89 Eagle Lane
Belle, MO, 65013

OAC
BOOKS
OSAGE ARTS COMMUNITY

First Edition1 3 5 7 9 10 8 6 4 2
ISBN: 978-1-950380-52-7
LCCN: 2019946938

Design, edits and layout: Jason Ryberg
Author photo: Matthew "Chigger" Haines

Acknowledgments:

The idea for this project began many years ago as a Middle School Science teacher. It wasn't until retirement that time and the ability to pull together the over 1300 items that resulted in this book.

Like any teacher, you have to be partially crazy, inventive, and an entertainer. Originally my students inspired me, unknowingly, in this endeavor. As I taught, I would sometimes switch the meanings of words to the questions they asked. This was sort like a walking Thesaurus. Sometimes corny but usually funny.

Finally, I started listening and writing them down. It was amazing how quickly they added up. It became a treasure trove of what people say that have strange meaning when strictly translated. It is no wonder why people from other countries have difficulty learning English.

This book has truly been a labor of love. I hope you enjoy reading it as much as I have writing it. Perhaps you will pass on your favorites.

This book could not have been written and completed without the valuable assistance of family and friends: Matthew Haines, Mimi Hedl, Barbara Huse, Cathy Manley, Mark McClane, Debbie Rowles, Jason Ryberg, Ann Scates, and my former students. My thanks is beyond words. Thank you!

-SV

TABLE OF CONTENTS

This book is dedicated to the two loves of my life,
my daughter Amber and my son Brock.

AGE

1. How do you know to act your age when you've never been this age before?

2. Who created the idea of the "fountain of youth?"

3. Did antiques exist in the olden days?

4. How old do you have to be before it can be said you died of old age?

5. When older people "roll a joint," is it their ankle?

6. Are you grown up when a nap is not a punishment but a reward?

7. How old does something have to be a "golden oldie?"

8. What happens when a "blast from the past" occurs?

9. When a person gets old, why do they put them "out to pasture?"

10. How far back do you need to go back to the "good old days?"

11. How is it that as you get older your father gets smarter?

AIRPLANES

1. Why don’t airplanes have horns?

2. Why don’t airplane bathrooms have windows?

3. Why do you need an airport if you’ve never had a plane land?

4. When airplane pilots are in training, do they take “crash courses?”

5. How do you get off a “nonstop” flight?

6. Do Kamikaze Pilots wear helmets?

7. Why is an airport a “terminal” if it is so safe?

8. If the black box flight recorder on an airplane is never damaged during a plane crash, why isn’t the airplane made of the same material?

9. What would Geronimo yell if he jumped out of an airplane?

10. Do pilots train to “fly by the seat of their pants?”

11. Does “onward and upward” only apply to astronauts and pilots?

12. Has anyone ever told a pilot to “straighten up and fly right?”

ANGER

1. If a salesman keeps calling and annoying you, should you give all the kids their phone number and tell them it's Santa's hotline?

2. If someone cuts you off in traffic, instead of flipping them off, should you get their license number and report their car stolen?

3. How do arguments hold water?

4. Instead of saying "top of the morning" to someone, do you say "bottom of the morning" to someone you dislike?

5. When you are upset, why do you "stew" about it?

6. Why do you tell someone to "hit the road?"

7. How do you "flip your lid" if you are mad?

8. When something comes to a finish, does it also "come to a head?"

9. Do you get "teed off" when you play golf?

10. If you do something in the "heat of the moment," should you wait until things "cool off?"

11. Where do you go when you get to "the end of the line?"

12. How do you "button your lip?"

13. Have you ever gone "ballistic?"

14. Why do we say we don't care until we have to?

15. Is there such a thing as a "civil" war?

16. Would it be a good idea "never to go to bed mad," but "stay up and plot your revenge"?

17. Why do we tell someone we are going to fire them and hire them cheaper, when they are a volunteer?

18. If you "lose your cool," where do you find it?

19. Why does someone tell you "in your face," when they think they have done something better than you?

20. Have you ever had a "chip" on your shoulder?

21. How do you get inside someone's face when they tell you to "get out of my face?"

22. Why do you tell someone to "get off my back?"

23. Have you ever seen anyone "thrown under a bus?"

24. What happens when you "get to the end of your rope?"

25. Have you ever cried over spilled milk?

26. When we are upset why do we have a "bone to pick?"

27. If you have been read the "riot act, what does it say?

28. How do you become "fit to be tied?"

29. Does someone really "have a cow" when they get mad?

30. Do you know anyone that has actually been "raked over the coals?"

31. Can a person really have a "meltdown" when they get mad?

32. How can someone go off "half- cocked?"

33. How do you get to the end of your wit, when you are at your "wit's end?"

34. When the tables are turned, do you really turn tables?

ANIMALS

1. Why doesn't Donald Duck have pants?

2. When will pigs fly?

3. When you are waist deep in alligators, is it hard to remember that your original intent was to drain the swamp?

4. Who first said, "I hope to kiss a pig?"

5. Why do dogs howl at the moon?

6. What made the cow jump over the moon?

7. Who keeps their ducks in a row?

8. Why do "birds of a feather" flock together?

9. Why should you never "look a gift horse in the mouth" even if horses don't give gifts?

10. Who figured out that you don't "put all of your eggs in one basket?"

11. Why does someone need to be told "not to put the cart in front of the horse?"

12. Why can't you teach an old dog new tricks, if you can teach a new dog old tricks?

13. Why do we wait for the "cows to come home?"

14. If Santa Claus is from the North Pole, where does the Easter Bunny come from?

15. How did the superstition that black cats are bad luck start?

16. What ever happened to Chicken Little?

17. Why does Prince Charming ride a white horse?

18. How can you get out-foxed?

19. Why isn't there a mouse flavored cat food?

20. How can someone be "part bloodhound?"

21. How do family members turn into "black sheep?"

22. If the early bird gets the worm, is it the second mouse that gets the cheese?

23. What do sheep count when they can't sleep?

24. If you throw a cat out the window, does it become "kitty litter?"

25. Do cows have "calf muscles?"

26. Who figured out "a bird in hand is worth two in the bush?"

27. Why would you want to lead a horse to water, if it's not going to drink?

28. Why do we count sheep when we can't sleep, instead of some other animal?

29. How do you "pet peeves?"

30. Have you ever seen a herd of turtles?

31. How do you become a "night owl?"

32. Does a veterinarian pull a "hen's teeth?"

33. Have you ever beat a "dead horse with a stick?"

34. Where do you find a "monkey business?"

35. What is a "pig in a poke?"

36. If some people are "meaner than a snake," how many snakes do you know?

37. How can a person be as "hungry as a bear?"

38. Have you ever acted "like a fish out of water?"

39. Have you ever seen a church mouse, to be able to tell if someone can be that quiet?

40. Have you ever been "as mad as a wet hen?"

41. Have you ever seen "a wolf in sheep's clothing?"

42. Have you ever seen an "elephant in a china closet?"

43. Have you ever been "as nervous as a long tail cat in a room full of rocking chairs?"

44. How do toads get strangled in a heavy rain?

45. How do you know if you are "dog tired?"

46. Is there anything "freer than a bird?"

47. Do little birdies tell you anything?

48. Are you a “lucky dog?”

49. Do you repel problems “like water off a duck’s back?”

50. Can you really “kill two birds with one stone?”

51. Why would you “let the cat out of the bag,” especially if you put it there in the first place?

52. How do you become “a cat’s meow?”

53. Is what is “good for the goose, good for the gander” true?

54. How do you become “sly as a fox?”

55. If you poured spot remover on your dog, Spot, would it disappear?

56. If there is “more than one way to skin a cat,” how many ways could there be?

57. Would you find “jumbo shrimp” in a sci-fi movie?

58. Did you ever have a dog people were upset with because they said "that dog won't hunt?

59. Has anyone tried "monkey see, monkey do?"

60. How often do you need to "get on your horse?"

61. How does a person get a "frog in their throat?"

62. How do you quit something "cold turkey?"

63. What happens when things "go to the dogs?"

64. Do frogs get "frogs in their throat?"

65. Do pigs pull their "hamstrings?"

66. If you put a chameleon in a room full of mirrors, what color would it turn?

67. Do sheep get static, when they rub against each other?

68. Can animals commit suicide?

69. Why do they call him "Donkey Kong" when he is not a donkey?

70. If a wool sweater shrinks when wet, why don't sheep shrink when they get wet?

71. Can something "get your goat" when you don't have a goat?

72. How can you be "loose as a goose?"

73. Who let the dogs out?

74. How do you get to be the pick of the litter?

75. Can a lamb "go on the lam?"

76. Have you ever seen anything that wild horses couldn't drag away?

77. Do dog "obedience schools" give homework?

78. Why do you "hold your horses," even if you don't have any horses?

79. Where do you get "horse sense?"

80. At dog obedience "schools" do people eat the dog's homework?

81. When someone tells you have a nice "hog" are they talking about your pig or your Harley?

82. Has anyone ever seen a straw "break a camel's back?"

BABIES

1. Why does the number of newborn deliveries increase during a full moon?

2. If peanut oil comes from peanuts, then what does "baby oil" come from?

3. Why would you have to tell someone "not to throw out the baby with the bath water?"

4. How do you "sleep like a baby?"

5. Would a baby be confused at a "topless bar?"

6. If a woman is expecting a baby, why is she said to "have a bun in the oven?"

7. If a baby is "spoiled rotten" should it be thrown away?

8. How is it possible to be born with a "silver spoon" in your mouth?

9. Why don't babies come with directions?

10. Why is a newborn baby called a "brand new baby?"

BASEBALL

1. Why do we sing "take me out to the ballgame" when we are already there?

2. Why isn't the foul pole in baseball called the "fair pole?"

3. If a baseball stops on the foul line, why is it called a fair ball?

4. Why are the places in the outfield where the relief pitchers sit called the "bullpen" instead of a relief pen?

5. When a pitcher is throwing hard, why is he said to be "bringing the heat?"

6. When a baseball is pitched close to the hitter, why is it said the ball is in his "kitchen?"

7. In baseball, could a "sacrifice fly" be a bug that is killed?

8. In baseball why does a "K" represent a strikeout?

9. How do you hit a baseball on the "screws?"

10. How can you "hit it out of the ballpark," when you are not playing baseball?

11. When a pitcher consistently throws hard and fast, why is he said to be "bringing the cheese?"

12. In baseball, how can a curveball "fall of the table," when no table is involved?

BEAUTY

1. Why is it called "beauty sleep," when you look terrible when you get up?

2. How can beauty be in the "eye of the beholder?"

3. If someone is as "cute as a button," is that really a compliment?

4. How can something be "pretty ugly?"

5. Why do you "tiptoe through the tulips?"

BUGS

1. Why is it called a "spelling bee," if bees can't spell?

2. Is the last thing that goes through a bug's mind when it hits a windshield its rear end?

3. What do you call a male ladybug?

4. Where did the saying "don't let the bed bugs bite" come from?

5. How tall do you need to be "knee high to a grasshopper?"

6. How can you be as "busy as a bee?"

7. How do you get "ants in your pants?"

8. How can someone be "a fly in the ointment?"

9. If a bee is allergic to pollen, would it get the hives?

10. Do butterflies remember life as a caterpillar?

11. Would you want to be a fly on the wall?

BUSINESS

1. If Fed Ex and UPS merged would it be called "FEDUPS?"

2. Why do you never hear about "gruntled" employees?

3. If "all the world is a stage," where does the audience sit?

4. Can electricians be "delighted?"

5. Can dry cleaners be "depressed?"

6. If you get cheated by the Better Business Bureau, who would you complain to?

7. A certain brand of soap is 99.9% pure what?

8. How do you become "the leader of the pack?"

9. Why are they called "apartments" if they are connected?

10. If a bald person is a chef at a restaurant, do they have to wear a "hairnet"?

11. Is there anything below the "bottom line?"

12. Is it easier to “go with the flow?”

13. Why are you asked to “keep a lid” on something?

14. What happens when you “have it covered?”

15. If you have “crossed the line” can you go back?

16. Do you keep things in “ship shape?”

17. How do you “fly under the radar?”

18. What are you when you can “take someone under your wing?”

19. What happens when you “get in over your head?”

20. What happens to the market, when you have it “cornered?”

21. Have you given anyone the choice of “your way or the highway?”

22. Once you “get the ball rolling,” how do you stop it?

23. Why would anyone tell you to “keep your pants on?”

24. When you are busy, why is it called “keeping a lot of balls in the air?”

25. What makes you “wet behind the ears?”

26. How do you keep something “all together” separate?

27. Why is it called a “friendly takeover?”

28. What is a “working vacation?”

29. When you “wrap it up,” what are you wrapping?

30. How did your job become compared to “working in the salt mines?”

31. How do you “hold down the fort?”

32. How do you “stay on track,” when no track is involved?

33. How “sharp” are you, if you are on the “cutting edge?”

34. Can you buy “fleas” at a flea market?

35. Is monkey business run by monkeys?

36. Why is your job referred to as a “rat race?”

37. If your business is very successful, why is it said that business is “through the roof?”

38. How many legs do waitresses hop on at “IHOP?”

39. Is there anything such as an “inconvenience store?”

40. Why is something “up your alley?”

41. If a store is open 24 hours a day, 365 days a year, why are there locks on the doors?

42. Why do you “throw the plan out the window,” when you start over?

43. How do you “blow away” the competition?

CEMETERIES

1. Is it hard to understand how a cemetery will raise its burial cost and blame it on the "cost of living?"

2. Should crematoriums offer discounts to burn victims?

3. Are people "dying" to get into cemeteries?

4. Do people who work in a cemetery prefer the "graveyard shift?"

CHURCHES

1. Why do churches have steeples?

2. Why does God help those who help themselves, but not those who get caught helping themselves?

3. Are atheists able to get insurance for "Acts of God?"

4. If God dropped acid would he see people?

5. What would you say if God sneezed?

6. Does a lightning rod on top of a church show lack of faith?

7. Why is there "no rest for the wicked?"

8. Can we do something so long as God is willing, even if the creek rises?

9. How can a blessing be disguised?

10. Do you know a "devilish angel?"

11. Have you ever met a "devout atheist?"

12. When Atheists go to court, do they have to swear on the Bible?

13. When someone says "holy smokes" are they in church?

14. How did "preaching to the choir" get started?

15. Are marriages really "made in heaven?"

16. If Michelangelo did the ceiling of the Sistine Chapel, who did the floor?

COLORS

1. Who gave the colors their names?

2. Why would someone say, "color me pink?"

3. Why is the grass always greener "on the other side?"

4. Why is silence "golden?"

5. What hair color is put on your driver's license if you are bald?

6. What color would a Smurf be if you choked it?

7. Is your favorite color "clear?"

8. Why was blue chosen if you are sad?

9. Do you really turn blue when you envy someone?

10. How can something be "clear as a bell?"

11. How can something be "clear as mud?"

12. Why is toilet bowl cleaner only blue?

13. If a woman dyes her hair blond, does she still have more fun?

14. Why are barns painted red?

15. Why do you "paint" the town red?

16. How can you "come through with flying colors?"

17. Why is snow white?

18. How do you "tickle someone pink?"

19. Why is an airplane's emergency recorder a "black box" when in fact it is orange?

DEATH

1. Should you worry about the end of the world, if it is already tomorrow in Australia?

2. Can a suicidal twin kill their twin by mistake?

3. What happens when you get "scared half to death" twice?

4. How important is someone, when it is said they have been assassinated instead of murdered?

5. If one synchronized swimmer drowns, do the rest of the swimmers drown also?

6. If someone with multiple personalities threatens suicide, can it be considered a hostage situation?

7. Why is the lid on a coffin locked?

8. Are there people willing to die to see someone that has died?

9. Even though it is said "hard work never killed anyone", why would you chance it?

10. How do you kill someone with "kindness?"

11. When you die, do you want your last words to be "I left a million dollars under the …?"

12. If you are dead, why are you "pushing up daisies?"

13. If you are drowning why would you "tread lightly?"

14. When you die, how do you "buy the farm?"

15. How do you "kick the bucket" when you die?

16. What does "death warmed over" look like?

17. Is it possible to "love someone to death?"

18. Why is a person in bad health said to "have one foot in the grave?"

19. Do people really eat a "dessert to die for?"

20. Have you ever been asked "who died and made you boss?"

21. Do you know anyone who has "died from embarrassment?"

22. In a "do or die" situation, if you don't do it do you really die?

23. If a funeral procession is at night, do the cars drive with their lights off?

24. Do coffins have lifetime guarantees?

25. Can zombies starve to death?

26. What is meant by "life in the balance?"

27. How can you have one foot in the grave and the other one on a banana peel?

28. Is there a difference between a ghost and a spirit?

29. Has anyone ever "died from laughing?"

DREAMS

1. If the future is "shaped by your dreams," should you just go to sleep?

2. Is it possible to "daydream" at night?

3. What does a "figment of your imagination" look like?

4. What is a "dream weaver?"

5. If you "follow your dreams," do you go back to bed?

6. When you have a "pipe dream" do you dream about pipes?

7. How can we have the "best of both worlds?"

8. Why are we told to "wake up and smell the coffee?"

9. How do you determine if you have a bad or "good head on your shoulders?"

10. Why is it some people can "tear up a dream?"

11. How do you make a "past prediction?"

12. How do people "live the dream?"

13. How do you "seize the day?"

14. Where does curiosity come from?

15. Why should you be careful what you wish for?

DRINKING

1. Why do drinking establishments have parking lots, if you can't "drink and drive?"

2. How can you be arrested for being "legally drunk?"

3. If a bouncer at a bar gets unruly, who throws him out?

4. Why is it called Alcoholics Anonymous, when the first thing you do at an AA meeting is to stand up and tell everyone you name?

5. If you are drunk after being sober, how do you "fall off the wagon?"

6. Why does someone say "here's mud in your eye" when taking a drink of alcohol?

7. How do you "drink someone under the table?"

8. Why are empty beer, wine, and whiskey cans and bottles called "dead soldiers?"

9. Why is it called "happy hour" when it lasts from 11 A.M. to 5 P.M.?

10. Why do you need a "belt," when you need an alcoholic drink?

11. Why do you get "plowed" or "plastered" when you drink too much?

12. Why have you had a "cup of coffee", when you have only been somewhere a short period of time?

13. Why don't people drink beer with a straw?

14. Why are you "hammered" if you are drunk?

DRIVING
AND
TRANSPORTATION

1. Why do we turn down the radio when we are driving and are lost or looking for an address?

2. Why is it called "rush hour" when we are stuck in traffic?

3. Why do race cars and horses go around a racetrack counterclockwise instead of clockwise?

4. Why do we park in driveways and drive on parkways?

5. Why is it called a "shipment" when you transport by car, but when transport by ship it is called "cargo?"

6. Will an elevator arrive faster if you push the button multiple times?

7. If most car accidents occur within five miles of home, why doesn't everyone move farther away?

8. How far to the East can you go before you're heading West?

9. Where did the saying "the train has left the station" come from?

10. Is the most dangerous part of a vehicle "the nut that holds the wheel?"

11. Why do you "spin your wheels?"

12. Why wouldn't you "cross that bridge when you come to it?"

13. Why would you need to "turn on a dime?"

14. Have you ever had the "rubber meet the road?"

15. If you are "firing on all cylinders" are you in a vehicle?

16. If you come to a "fork in the road" do you take it?

17. How do you know you are "on the right track?"

18. How can you be "going" nowhere?

19. Where do you find an "elevated subway?"

20. If a taxi cab driver would drive backwards, would he end up owing the passenger money?

21. Can a hearse, carrying a corpse drive in the carpool lane?

22. When cars run off the road, why are they attracted to trees or telephone poles?

23. Why is a semi-truck trailer 53 feet long?

24. How do you get a "sweet ride?"

25. If a VIP asks for a "driver," are they in a limousine or playing golf?

26. How do you get to the "middle of nowhere?"

27. What mode of transportation do use to "get up to speed?"

EDUCATION

1. Why is the "pen mightier than the sword?"

2. What set of Siamese twins decided "two heads are better than one?"

3. When a little bit of knowledge is a dangerous thing, is a lot of knowledge "catastrophic?"

4. Could the difference between a stupid person and a genius be that genius has limits?

5. Is education what is left over after we have forgotten what we have learned in school?

6. Did man invent language to satisfy his need to complain?

7. How smart do you have to be to be "smarter than a fox?"

8. Have you ever seen anyone drink at the "fountain of knowledge?"

9. Why don't we have a "fountain of smart?"

10. Do you do your homework while the teacher is collecting it?

11. Do intelligent people have messier handwriting because they think faster?

12. If you read too many books can you turn into a bookworm?

13. How do you become "sharp as a tack?"

14. When you are "spot on" where are you?

15. How does something "dawn on you?"

16. Where is the "school of hard knocks" located?

17. How do become a "smart cookie?"

18. How do you get to be the "cream of the crop?"

19. How can your "intelligence be insulted?"

20. How do you make an "educated guess?"

21. If you speak only one language are you lingual?

22. Do you have to be in college to give the "old college try?"

23. How do you become "smart as a whip?"

24. Is someone considered a "genius" because they see things before they happen?

25. What happens when your brain gets full?

26. What agency oversees "spoiler alerts?"

EXPLOSIONS

1. Why does dynamite come in small packages?

2. How do you get "blown away?"

3. If you are "blown away," do you come back?

4. How do you "rock your world?"

5. How was it determined that it was bad to have your "bubble burst?"

6. How do you "blow" things out of proportion?

7. How can something "knock your socks off?"

FIGHTING

1. When you are told to "turn the other cheek," which cheek do you turn?

2. When you divide anything, is it always conquered?

3. How do you "sweat bullets?"

4. Who first discovered that "to the victor go the spoils?"

5. How do you "make heads roll?"

6. How do you "wrestle" with a problem?

7. If a crime fighter fights crime and a fire fighter fights fire, what does a "freedom fighter" fight?

8. Can it take more than "two to tango?"

9. Do you "pick your battles?"

10. When you "give someone the boot," which boot do you give them?

11. What is the point of "raising the roof?"

12. If you "come out swinging," what are you trying to hit?

13. When the "going gets tough," why do the "tough get going?"

14. Why do we say a person has an "axe to grind" when they have a problem with something?

15. Why are you said to be "stirring the pot" when you cause a conflict?

16. Why do we "fight to the finish?"

17. Have you ever been in a "fight that you didn't have a dog in?"

18. Why do we "agree to disagree?"

19. Have you ever "knocked someone's block off?"

20. How do you fight "tooth and nail?"

21. How do you get "fit to be tied?"

22. How do you "roll with the punches?"

23. Can dueling be legal so long as both parties are registered blood donors?

FIRE

1. Why do you "strike while the iron is hot?"

2. What happens if you put "too many irons in the fire?"

3. Who discovered "if you play with fire you will get burned?"

4. If you ever catch on fire, why would you look in a mirror?

5. How can one careless match start a forest fire, and yet it takes a whole box of matches to start a campfire?

6. Have you ever seen a "worm in hot ashes?"

7. If a candle factory caught fire, would the employees stand around and sing Happy Birthday?

8. Why would someone "add fuel to the fire?"

9. Why would you want to "hold your feet to the fire?"

10. How do you get put on the "hot seat?"

FOOD

1. Why is dishwashing liquid made with real lemons and lemon juice is made with artificial substitutes?

2. Why is it called "chili" if it's hot?

3. Why do schools have "free lunch" programs if there is no such thing as a "free lunch?"

4. Why is it said that a "watched pot never boils," when we know it will eventually?

5. Why would you "bite the hand that feeds you?"

6. Who makes lemonade when "life gives you a lemon?"

7. Why doesn't the apple ever fall far from the tree?

8. Why can't you "have your cake and eat it too?"

9. If we are not supposed to eat at night, why is there a light in the refrigerator?

10. Are "animal" crackers eaten by "vegetarians?"

11. If vegetarians eat vegetables, what do humanitarians eat?

12. Is it true that cannibals don't eat clowns because they taste funny?

13. If a "parsley" farmer is sued, do they "garnish" his wages?

14. Do Lipton tea employees take coffee breaks?

15. Why does a round pizza get delivered in a square box?

16. Why is it people eat natural food and still die from natural causes?

17. What do people in China call their "good plates?"

18. What was best before sliced bread?

19. Why doesn't McDonald's sell hotdogs?

20. How fast do hotcakes sell?

21. Does the "sweet taste of victory" taste sweet?

22. Why do green olives come in jars, but black olives come in cans?

23. What “proof is in the pudding?”

24. How can people be like “two peas in a pod?”

25. What makes something “peachy?”

26. How does someone become “the apple of your eye?”

27. Are you really what you eat?

28. Why is it called a “pie chart” when it has nothing to do with pies?

29. If you turn into a “couch potato” are you considered a carbohydrate?

30. Do you share your food because you love to share or because it fell on the floor?

31. Have you ever seen a “pie in the sky?”

32. Does “cleaning your plate” include scraping the food off onto the table?

33. Why do people “bite off more than they can chew?”

34. Why do we take things with a “grain of salt?”

35. How can something be “easy as pie?”

36. Can you be “full as a tick?”

37. How do “too many cooks spoil the pot?”

38. Can something be a “hot potato” even if is not a potato?

39. What happens when you “take the cake?”

40. When someone talks about “leaving meat on the bone,” are they really talking about meat or selling an antique?

41. Who discovered “life is a bowl of cherries?”

42. Why did Yankee Doodle stick a feather in his cap and call it macaroni?

43. Where can you find the “whole enchilada?”

44. How can something be “awfully good?”

45. Where do you get “food for thought?”

46. Does a “free market economy” mean you can go to the grocery store and get your food for free?

47. How do you "whet" your appetite?"

48. If tuna is sometimes called "tuna fish," why isn't chicken called "chicken bird?"

49. What spot is hit, when it "hits the spot?"

50. If you are "subconscious" are you conscious about sub sandwiches?

51. If you are the "toast of the town" are you made of bread?

52. Why do people "chew the fat?"

53. How can you be a "bad egg" if you are not an egg?

54. How do you "relish" a thought?

55. How do you "get egg on your face?"

56. Can a bad apple really "spoil the bunch?"

57. How do you become a "bad apple"?

HAPPINESS

1. How do you establish a "comfort zone?"

2. Why isn't everything "sunshine and roses?"

3. How do you become a "happy camper?"

4. How do you become "bright eyed and bushy tailed?"

5. How can humor be "dry?"

6. How can you be "happy as a clam?"

7. How do you find out if "happy wife, happy life" is true?

HEARING

1. If blind people wear dark glasses, why don't deaf people wear earplugs?

2. Is it still called a "hearing" when a deaf person goes to court?

3. Can musicians be denoted?

4. Why do you never hear father-in-law jokes?

5. How do you "play something by ear?"

6. Why is it called a soap "opera" when nobody sings?

7. Why would someone tell you to "keep your ears open," if it's not possible to close your ears?

8. Have you ever seen someone that is "all ears?"

9. What do you hear when "opportunity knocks?"

10. How can actions "speak" louder than words?

11. What do you hear when you "hear it from the grapevine?"

12. Why do you "put your ear to the ground?"

13. Do you ever "listen with a tin whistle?"

14. When you are told to "zip it" what do you zip?

15. How many times have you said, it "sounded" like a good idea at the time?

16. Why do you "jump on the bandwagon" if you are not part of a band?

17. If you have trouble with something going in one ear and out the other, should you put a finger in one of your ears?

18. Can you be a "deaf listener?"

19. Where do you find "deafening silence?"

20. If a deaf child signs swear words, does his mother wash his hands with soap?

21. Why would you want to arrive somewhere with "bells and whistles on?"

22. How much does it take to "get an earful?"

HEART

1. Why do we do something "to our heart's desire?"

2. How do you mend a "broken heart?"

3. How do you put your "heart and soul" into something?

4. When you are trying to get to the "heart of the matter," will you really find a heart?

HONESTY

1. Who determined that "honesty is the best policy?"

2. How do you "save face" and what are saving it for?

3. How do you "keep someone honest?"

4. Does everyone subscribe to the idea "ask me no questions and I will tell you no lies?"

5. Do you always "reap what you sow?"

6. What happens when you "put it all on the table?"

7. Why do you "toe the line?"

8. When you make your bed, do you have to lie on it?

9. Why are your "lips sealed?

10. If something can be "fair game," can it be unfair also?

11. What happens when you "hit the nail on the head?"

12. How do you make something "fair and square?"

13. When you "make a point" is it sharp?

14. What happens when you "spill the beans?"

15. If you speak the "plain truth" can the truth be "unplain?"

16. Does a "whistle blower" use a whistle?

17. Why do people "play both ends against the middle?"

18. If a person told you that they were a "pathological liar" would you believe them?

19. How do we "face the truth?"

20. How does "the wool get pulled over your eyes?"

21. Is it better to be "slapped with the truth" than "kissed with a lie?"

22. Why is something done "accidently on purpose?"

23. Do you know any "doubting believers?"

24. How can a lie be "white?"

25. Have you ever "stacked the deck?"

26. How do you "lie through your teeth?"

27. How do you "sandbag" someone?

28. Why is the term "come clean" about honesty and not cleanliness?

29. Why is it important to "stay on the straight and narrow?"

30. Why is it said that you are "blowing smoke" when you are not telling the truth?

31. How do you know when you have reached the "moment of truth?"

32. Why does someone "pull your leg?"

INJURIES

1. Why is it the "bigger they are, the harder they fall on you?"

2. Is everything better than a "poke in the eye?"

3. When you have your "bell rung" how long does it ring?

4. Have you ever "dodged a bullet?"

5. Are "bullet points" harmful?

6. Do you know anyone who had "their eye shot out" playing with a weapon?

7. Do you become "head over heels" when you slip or trip or are in love?

8. Have you seen anything that "cost an arm and a leg?"

9. Why would you add "insult to injury?"

10. Does it hurt when you "keep your nose to the grindstone?"

11. Does it hurt when you "put yourself through the wringer?"

12. When you come to a "slippery slope" do you go around it?

13. Have you been seriously sick or injured and told that you "were not out of the woods" yet?"

14. Why would you "cut off your nose to spite your face?"

15. Does "painless torture" exist?

16. How can you give society a black eye?

17. What causes someone to "fall apart," even though they stay in one piece?

INSANITY

1. Why do we do something "after the fact?"

2. If nothing is going right, should you go left?

3. Why do we do the same thing over and over and expect different results?

4. Do you find that when everything is coming your way, you're in the wrong lane and going the wrong way?

5. Why do psychics have to ask your name?

6. Isn't being "caught between a rock and a hard place" the same thing?

7. How can something be "scary good?"

8. Can you put a gay person in a strait jacket?

9. Why are some good ideas "insane?"

10. Do you know anyone whose elevator doesn't go all the way to the top?

11. Who said, "you can't fix crazy?"

12. Have you ever figured out that some people need a shock collar and you want the controls?

13. Where do you find that line that separates reality from fantasy?

14. If you always find what you are looking for in the last place you look, should you look there first?

15. Why do we ask someone for a match when their arms are full?

16. Why is someone who is crazy called a "looney tune?"

17. If you are crazy do you have "bats in the belfry?"

18. How do you get "higher than a kite?"

19. Is there a "method to your madness?"

20. Have you ever "taken leave of your senses?"

21. If you don't suffer from insanity, do you enjoy every minute of it?

22. How can you tell if someone is "one brick shy of a load?"

23. Can something become "insane logic?"

24. Can "organized chaos" be real?

25. When crazy people walk through the forest, do they take the psycho path?

26. Why do superheroes wear their underwear on the outside of their clothes?

27. If someone is crazy, why is it said that no one is home?

28. How do you "toast someone" when they are too big for the toaster?

29. If you are crazy, did you really "lose your marbles?"

30. How do you become "nutty as a fruitcake?"

INVENTION

1. Why hasn't anyone invented a trash compactor for cars?

2. Why does the "squeaky wheel" always get the grease?

3. Why would you try to "fix something if it's not broke?"

4. Why is necessity the "mother" of invention?

5. Before drawing boards, were invented, what did people go back to?

6. How can you tell if you are out of invisible ink?

7. Why do we call it a hot water heater when it heats cold water and should be called a cold-water heater?

8. What appeared above people's heads before the light bulb was invented?

9. Why do overalls have belt loops?

10. If something is "out of whack" what does it take to make it in whack?

11. How often do you "think outside the box?"

12. Are you describing a boomerang when you say, "what goes around comes around?"

13. Who invented "non-stick glue?"

14. Who invented paper table "cloths?"

15. Who invented "wireless" cable?

16. Have you ever seen a "lead balloon?"

17. Who invented plastic "glasses?"

18. How do you make a "security blanket?"

19. How ironic is it that the first toilet was invented by Thomas Crapper?

20. Why are there no "B" batteries?

21. Is it good or bad if a vacuum sweeper really "sucks"?

22. Who invented the "science of persuasion?"

23. When something doesn't work, why do you go back to "square one?"

JUDGING

1. Why can't you "judge a book by its cover?"

2. Is it possible for a short person to "talk down" to a taller person?

3. Have you found no one listens until you make a mistake?

4. How does someone become a "chip off the old block?"

5. Is patience what you have when there are too many witnesses?

6. If people are trying to "bring you down," does that mean you are above them?

7. Does everyone "do as I say and not as I do?"

8. Why would you "throw someone a bone?"

9. Why does it "take one to know one?"

10. What happens when you get to "the last straw?"

11. If you are "two faced" does that mean you could be Dr. Jekyll and Mr. Hyde?

12. Has anyone ever threatened to "hunt you down like the dog you are?"

13. How do you "cut to the chase?"

14. Does your name have to Thomas to be a "doubting Thomas?"

15. How do you "open a can of worms?"

16. If you witness a "jaw dropping" event, how would you pick it up?

17. How do you "make a mountain out of a mole hill?"

18. Can something be "better than new?"

19. Can a "partial" conclusion be reached?

20. Why would you "dare to compare?"

21. How do you get "on the fence?"

22. How do you "face the music?"

23. How do you "wear out your welcome?"

24. Why would you wear "the shoe on the other foot?"

25. What causes a "gut feeling?"

THE LAW

1. Do they tell a mime he has the right to speak, if he is arrested?

2. Why are we considered to be in "hot water" when we are in trouble?

3. If it is "tourist season" can they be hunted and shot?

4. If it is illegal to scream fire in a theater, is it illegal to scream theatre in a fire?

5. Why aren't lawyers sworn in?

6. Why don't they put photos of the FBI's 10 most wanted criminals on postage stamps?

7. Does a person get put on a railroad when they get "railroaded?"

8. Did you ever tell yourself "it's not worth the jail time?"

9. When you want to slap a person, do you go ahead and do it and yell mosquito?

10. What gave Murphy the right to make his own law?

11. If you step on a cornflake, does that make you a cereal killer?"

12. Why do we use the term "catch and release" when fishing, when you could use the same term for our judicial system?

13. How do you get "behind the eight 8 ball?"

14. How do "five finger discounts" become available?

15. What happens when you "get to the bottom of something?"

16. Do you discard the small fish if you "have bigger fish to fry?"

17. Have you ever "burned bridges?"

18. If you are surrounded by the "fuzz," do you need a shave?

19. Do you deal with a "common criminal" the same way you would deal with one that was "uncommon?"

20. Have you ever "had the book thrown at you?"

21. Could it be true that some people are alive only because it is illegal to kill them?

22. Have you ever had a "tough nut to crack?"

23. When "the worm has turned," which direction does it go?

24. Have you ever seen a "genuine fake?"

25. What causes someone to be "scared stiff?"

26. What kind of legal issue is involved when "the ball is in your court?"

27. If you steal a clean slate, does it go on your record?

28. Is it legal to drive down a road in reverse, if you are following the direction of travel?

29. Who gets to be king if a queen gives birth to Siamese twin boys?

30. How do you get left "holding the bag?"

31. How do you "buck the system?"

32. Did God make snakes before he made lawyers because he needed practice?

33. Does the Second Amendment really give us the right to "bear" (give birth to) arms?

34. Is advice "only worth what you pay for it?"

35. Why is it said, "you made your bed, now you must lie in it?"

36. Why is something "hung out to dry," when it is not laundry?

37. How do you "get off the hook," when no hook is involved?

LAZINESS

1. Why does it take less to do something right the first time than to do it over?

2. If you did nothing yesterday, would you finish it today?

3. If you won an award for laziness, would you send someone else to pick it up?

4. If you get excited about canceling your plans are you considered lazy?

5. How do we earn the chance to be given a second chance?

6. Have you ever made a large to do list and then couldn't figure out who was going to do it?

7. Are the first five days after the weekend the hardest?

8. If your boss told you to have a good day would you go home?

9. Why do some people "drop the ball?"

10. Why are some people said to "mail it in" when they don't want to do their job?

11. Why do some people "talk the talk," but can't "walk the walk?"

12. When not doing anything, why don't you have to lift a finger?

13. How can someone just "skate" by?

14. How many people do you know that want a job, but don't want to work?

15. What is the difference between "goofing around" and "goofing off?"

16. Is there such a thing as "planned spontaneity?"

17. Why is watching golf for some people like watching grass grow?

18. Why do you lose if you "snooze?"

19. Why are we waiting for "Hell to freeze over" before we do something?

LIGHT

1. Is the speed of light the same as the speed of darkness?

2. Why is there a light in the refrigerator but not in the freezer?

3. Is the light at the end of the tunnel always a train?

4. Why is it darkest before dawn?

5. What happens when you "shed some light" on something?

LOVE
AND
APPRECIATION

1. Is "all is fair in love and war" true?

2. Is "absence makes the heart grow fonder" true?

3. Is it always lonely at the top?

4. If love is blind, can marriage be an eye opener?

5. Can you be left alone with your own devices?

6. What is "French kissing" called in France?

7. If love is blind, why is lingerie so popular?

8. If you feel unappreciated, should you compare yourself to a white crayon?

9. If you think no one cares if you are alive, should you try missing several payments?

10. Have you ever felt like a "lonely petunia?"

11. When you love someone, why do you "carry a torch" for them?

12. How can you be "legal to a fault?"

13. Have you ever been "taken for granted?"

14. How can you "love someone to pieces?"

15. When you are told to "take care of someone", does that mean you have to kill them?

MEANINGS AND SEMANTICS

1. If nothing is impossible, is it possible for something to be impossible?

2. Does a reverse side also have a reverse side?

3. Why is it called the "Department of Interior" when it oversees all things outdoors for the U.S. government?

4. Why do we put "garments" in a suitcase and "suits" in a garment bag?

5. What is the difference between a "slim chance" and a "fat chance?"

6. If "I am" is the shortest sentence in the English language is "I do" the longest?

7. What does "PU" stand for if something stinks?

8. If there is an exception to every rule, is there an exception to that rule?

9. When a French person swears, do they say, "pardon my English?"

10. Why do "unthaw" and "thaw" mean the same thing?

11. Why aren't tugboats called "push boats" since they push and don't tug?

12. "To each his own" what?

13. Why is something "nothing to sneeze at?"

14. If we can be "laid back," can we also "stand forward?"

15. Is a "hairy situation" hairy?

16. If you "can't stand the heat," why should you stay out of the kitchen?

17. Can you fly when you "wing it?"

18. If you "cut ties," do you still wear suits?

19. How do you get "beside the point?"

20. Are you talking about a monster's well-being when discussing "creature comforts?"

21. Do you have a "least favorite?"

22. Have you ever observed "obedient defiance?"

23. How do make a "parallel connection?"

24. How can something have "freezer burn?"

25. How do you "get real?"

26. If something is "over the top," what is it over the top of?

27. Do people dating in the Netherlands go "English" instead of "Dutch?"

28. What happens to an irresistible force when it hits an immovable object?

29. Why is it called "raw sewage?"

30. If you had a three-story house and you were on the second floor, isn't possible that you can be upstairs and downstairs at the same time?

31. Why does "slow down" and "slow up" mean the same thing?

32. Why are sewer cover plates called "manhole covers?"

33. How does something become a "humdinger?"

34. How do you leave with “your tail between your legs” when you don’t have a tail?

35. What does it mean to be “back in the day?”

36. When someone tells you to “hang on,” what do hang on to and for how long?

37. If a person has a weapon, why are they “armed?”

38. When you get a different home, why is it referred to as your “new digs?”

39. Can you have a “private” conversation, even if you’re not in the Army?

40. Why is the front of a clock or watch called the “face?”

41. How do you “push” the envelope?

42. Why do we “scale” both a mountain and a fish?

43. When you ask for a “driver,” are you playing golf or asking for a chauffeur?

44. How do you know whether you are “on the same page” or not?

45. Do you have to be a "one timer" before you can become a "two-timer?"

46. Why is it called a "building," when it is already built?

47. Why do you "hit the nail on the head" when you are correct?

48. How do you get a "feel for something?"

49. Why is a blemish in nylon stockings called a "run?"

50. If you like something, why do you "dig" it?

MEDICINE

1. Why do we state, “it’s a bitter pill to swallow?”

2. Why do we take pills if “laughter is the best medicine?”

3. How does “an apple a day keep the doctor away” work?

4. Does it make you nervous to know your doctor has a “practice?”

5. How confident would you be if you found out your surgeon graduated last in his class?

6. If 4 out of 5 people suffer from diarrhea, does it mean that one enjoys it?

7. Why does your nose “run” and your feet “smell?”

8. Why do they sterilize the needle before “lethal” injections?

9. Why is it called a “funny bone,” when it’s not funny when you hit it?

10. Do bald people get dandruff?

11. If you have the "guts to do something," does it take a lot of intestines?

12. Can you be "allergic" to water?

13. Who measures the "pulse of the nation?"

14. If athletes get "athlete's foot," do astronauts get "missile toe?"

15. Who came up with "that's no skin off my nose?"

16. Who first described something as "slick as snot?"

17. Have you ever been "sick as a dog?"

18. How is it you give someone "a real shot in the arm?"

19. When you are "up to par" are you golfing?

20. How can something be "icy hot?"

21. How do you give someone "a taste of their own medicine?"

THE MIND

1. How do we know "great minds think alike?"

2. If we tell people the brain is an app, will they start using it?

3. How do you give someone a "piece of your mind?"

4. Is it possible to have too much on your mind for what mind you have left?

5. Is a "clear conscious" a sign of a bad memory?

6. If you have an "open mind," will your brains fall out?

7. If it is "out of sight" can it be "out of mind?"

8. What keeps everything from happening at once?

9. How do you get "peace of mind?"

10. What determines how you "make up your mind?"

11. If something "blows your mind," can you put the pieces back together?

12. How do you have a "meeting of the minds?"

13. Do you have a mind like a "steel trap?"

14. What happens when something "slips your mind?"

15. Do you consider yourself a "legend in your own mind", instead of a "legend in your own time"?

16. When something is in the "back of your mind," what is in the front?

17. Does a "no brainer' occur when there is no brain?

18. Does your brain was "cash" checks you can't cash?

19. What happens when you "rack your brain?"

20. If you "lose your mind," how do you find it again?

21. How do you take something "off the top of your head?"

22. If "mind over matter" is true, then if you have no mind then it doesn't matter also true?

23. When you "clear your mind" is it vacant?

24. How do you get a "brain freeze?"

25. Is it possible to be "mentally bankrupt?"

26. How do you "mind your P's and Q's?"

27. How do you "wrap your brain" around something?

28. Where do you get "fuel for thought?"

29. How can a brain get "fried?"

MONEY

1. If you get caught when you “pinch a penny”, do you go to jail?

2. Why do coins have ridges?

3. Why does a “Canadian” two-dollar bill have an “American flag” flying over the Parliament building?

4. Why can’t beggars be choosers?

5. Who discovered it doesn’t cost anything to wish?

6. How much “bang” do you get for a buck?

7. Why is it said, “money doesn’t bring happiness,” while everyone still wants to prove it for themselves?

8. Why don’t wallets come with free refills?

9. Why are the “best things in life free?”

10. Why do banks have “branches” if money doesn’t grow on trees?

11. Why are there Braille dots on the pad of drive up ATM’s?

12. Is the quickest way to "double" your money to fold it in half?

13. If Barbie is so popular, why do you have to purchase all of her friends?

14. Do you give someone a "penny" when they are not worth "two cents?"

15. Why are there phone bills in a country of free speech?

16. Why is the person who invests your money called a "broker?"

17. Can you purchase an entire chess set in a "pawn" shop?

18. If a criminal turns himself in, should they get the reward money?

19. Are you overpaying when you give "a penny for your thoughts" and you "give them two cents worth?"

20. How do you "coin" a phase?

21. Who realized that your “signature and a dollar” would get you a cup of coffee?

22. Who determines when “there is a price to pay” for doing something?

23. Why can’t money buy happiness?

24. What happens when you tell someone “to show me the money” and they are broke?”

25. Is work something you do until you win the lottery?

26. Why are items “cheaper by the dozen?”

27. When you “borrow trouble,” how do you pay it back?

28. How do you measure the “price of victory?”

29. Why doesn’t money grow on trees?

30. What happens when someone “pays the price?”

31. Do you die if you become “dead broke?”

32. If money grew on trees, would you buy a forest?

33. Have you ever been so poor you couldn't "pay attention?"

34. How often has someone "laughed at your expense?"

35. How can you be "right on the money?"

36. Does everyone wait for their "ship to come in?"

37. Do "gold diggers" really dig for gold?

38. Did you ever want to be a banker, but then you lost "interest?"

39. How can there be "abundant poverty?"

40. How can "deficits rise?"

41. How do you make a "safe bet?"

42. How can you have a "zero deficit?"

43. Is "one man's trash" always someone's treasure?

44. Why does a "priceless" object cost more than a pricey one?

45. Can you stop payment on a "reality check?"

46. If you don't pay your exorcist, do you get "repossessed?"

47. Where can you find a dozen for a dime?

48. How can so many banks claim to be First banks?

49. Why do a fool and his money soon separated?

50. Are you working on your second million dollars because you gave up on the first one?

51. Why is money called "dough?"

52. How can you be like "two sides of the same coin?"

53. How do you become "strapped" for money?

54. Why aren't shorts half the price of long pants?

55. When you owe someone money, why would tell them you would "pay them back as soon as you can" when you can't pay them back sooner?

56. Is it true that the term "buck," which is slang for money, came from trading buckskins during pioneer days?

57. Why do you "put your money where your mouth is"?

58. How can something be "right on the money", when no money is involved?

NUMBERS AND LETTERS

1. Why are wrong phone numbers never busy?

2. Why is “two company and three is a crowd”?

3. Why are we scared of the number 13, if it hasn’t been unlucky to us?

4. How can there be three kinds of people, those that can count and those that can’t?

5. If the #2 pencil is the most popular, why is it still #2?

6. Who decided the order of the alphabet?

7. Where do you find the four corners of the Earth?

8. If you are in “7th Heaven,” what happened to the other six?

9. Why does a baker’s dozen equal 13?

10. If someone does something twice are they a two-timer?”

11. If plan A fails, do you remember there are 25 letters left?

12. Why is "1" the loneliest number?

13. Is "hindsight always 20/20?"

14. How is the "credibility gap" measured?

15. Why is it called the "whole nine yards?"

16. Why do you "mark your words?"

17. If someone "has your 6," who has 1-5?

18. When people "count on you," what number do they start with?

19. When you are told to "take five," what five things do you take?

20. How do you put something in "random order?"

21. What is a "single pair?"

22. How do you determine what is the "larger half?"

23. If a word is misspelled in a dictionary, how would anyone know?

24. Why are numbers on a calculator and a phone reversed?

25. Is there another name for "thesaurus?"

26. Why do we expect more for less?

27. If something is a "catch-22," what happened to the first 21 catches?

28. How do you "read" lips?

PEOPLE

1. Why do men try to assemble an item without reading the directions first?

2. Why doesn't Tarzan need to shave like other men?

3. If the Pilgrims came to the New World, then where did the Indians come from?

4. Why is someone considered an expert because they live 100 miles away?

5. What happens when people "push your buttons?"

6. If you are hotter than me, does that make me cooler than you?

7. Why does the TV ask if you know where your children are?

8. When people text "call me" should you call them and when they answer say "text me" and hang up?

9. What happened to the "last of the Mohicans?"

10. Can you tell that sex was so great, even the neighbors had a cigarette?

11. If you spin an “Oriental” person around, do they become “disoriented?”

12. What do you call a male ballerina?

13. Do Mermaids wear “algebras?”

14. Can cowboys be “deranged?”

15. Why are a “wise guy” and a “wise man” opposite?

16. Why do we recite in plays and play in recitals?

17. Why is the person that plays the piano a “pianist,” but a race car driver is not a “racist?”

18. Is it possible to plan a surprise birthday party for a psychic?

19. Does anyone vanish “with a trace?”

20. If Hooters were to become a door to door service would they change their name to “Knockers?”

21. How do you “make a believer” out of someone?

22. How do you “let someone down” if they are not higher than you?

23. How can you tell if blondes really “have more fun?”

24. What happens when someone tells you to “shake a leg” and you can't?

25. How can a person be “fair to middling`?”

26. Is a “happy medium” a pleased psychic?

27. What is a “local yokel?”

28. How often do you “reach out and touch someone?”

29. Have you “never met a stranger?”

30. Would you call yourself a “diamond in the rough?”

31. How do you “set yourself apart?”

32. How can someone be “alone in a crowd?”

33. Can someone be an “intimate stranger?”

34. Can someone be “found missing?”

35. Should “dumpster diving” be an Olympic event?

36. Do married people really live longer than a single person, or does it just seem that way?

37. Does the mailman deliver his own mail?

38. Do stuttering people stutter when they are thinking to themselves?

39. Can an ambidextrous person make an offhand remark?

40. Do people in Hell tell other people where to go?

41. Are children who use sign language allowed to talk with their mouths full?

42. What do Greeks say when they don’t understand something?

43. When you go through a checkout lane, do you check out the cashier?

44. If you second guess someone, have you already first guessed them?

45. Do you "wear the pants" in your family?

46. Do you have to be named Johnny to be "Johnny on the spot?"

47. How do you get the "right people on the bus?"

48. What is the difference between a janitor and a custodian?

49. If you "put people down" do you raise them up also?

50. How can you tell people are "worth their salt?"

51. How do you determine a person's "strong suit?"

52. How do you develop the "patience of a saint?"

53. Can someone really "vanish into thin air?"

54. Are people "put out to pasture?"

55. Why do people "march to the beat of their own drum?"

56. When someone asks you to give them "a hand," why do you applaud?

57. Does your last name have to be McCoy for you to be a "Real McCoy?"

58. How do people "dance to their own tune?"

59. Does a taxidermist get "stuffed" at Thanksgiving?

60. Do cowboys ever utter a "discouraging word?"

61. When you call "toll free," why does someone with a different name answer the phone?

62. Can a person be "tickled silly?"

63. Are "skeleton staffs" skeletons?

64. If someone has your "back," who has your "front?"

65. Do you have to be named Steven to make things "even Steven?"

PICTURES

1. Why is a picture "worth a thousand words?"

2. When you take a photo of cheese what does it say?

3. How can you "draw a blank?"

4. How can you be a "picture of good health?"

5. Why do we say "cheese" when we have our picture taken?

6. How does something become "picture perfect?"

7. How do you "paint a rosy picture?"

8. Is your picture on a poster, if someone tells you they will "keep you posted?"

9. How can you be "framed" if you are not a picture?

10. Do pictures of "runaway" trains appear on the sides of milk cartons?

PLANTS

1. Is a paper cut a tree's "final revenge?"

2. Can tree surgeons be "debarked?"

3. Do all mechanics need a "shade tree?"

4. How can you feel "fresh as a daisy?"

5. Where are you when you "can't see the forest for the trees?"

6. How "cool" is a cucumber?

7. How do we "bark up the wrong tree?"

8. Can there be a "giant dwarf?"

9. If a tree crashes in a forest, how do we know it makes a noise?

10. How do you turn over a "new leaf?"

11. Why is a factory called a "plant?"

POLITICS

1. Why do you “throw your hat in the ring” if you are running for political office?

2. Is it possible to succeed in politics when you find it necessary to “rise above your principles?”

3. Could the problem with “political jokes” be that they get elected?

4. Why would you do something at a “drop of a hat?”

5. Why would you “walk on eggshells?”

6. Why do politicians “kick the can down the road?”

7. How does something react when they “give it a shot?”

8. What happens when the “worm has turned?”

9. Should you be kind to the people on the way to the top, just in case you pass them on the way back down?

10. Where are you when you “meet in the middle?”

11. Have you ever been a part of the “changing of the guard?”

12. What are you doing when you are "in the thick of it?"

13. Are politicians good at "direct circumvention?"

14. If pros and cons are opposite, wouldn't the opposite of progress be congress?

15. Are there fatalities in a "trade war?"

16. Do politicians "take the heat?"

17. Why is it in politics, if you want a friend you should get a dog?

18. How do you "let your actions do the talking?"

POTENTIAL

1. Why do we call an action the "name of the game?"

2. How do you "rise to the occasion?"

3. Instead of being "the best you can be" why don't people try to "be better than they can be?"

4. What happens when you "miss the mark?"

5. How do you get to be at the "bottom of the totem pole?"

6. How can there be a "definite maybe?"

SAFETY

1. Why would you "leap before you look?"

2. When you are told "not to try this at home," should you instead try it somewhere else?"

3. Why is it said someone "shot themselves in the foot" when they didn't really shoot themselves?

4. Why is it said that something is "an accident waiting for a place to happen?"

5. Have you ever seen a ship sunk by "loose lips?"

6. Why would you take a "shot in the dark?"

7. When taking a risk, are you "out on a limb?"

8. Why do we tell someone to "break a leg" before they make a performance?

9. Do you know anyone with "two left feet?"

10. If Superman could stop bullets with his body, why did he duck when someone threw a gun at him?

11. Why do you have to wait for someone to give you a "green light" to be able to do something?

SAYINGS

1. Who came up with the saying "different strokes for different folks?"

2. Why can't it be over until the "fat lady sings?"

3. Why are the rows "long to hoe?"

4. Why do we call it AC-DC instead of DC-AC?

5. Why does it all "come out in the wash?"

6. How do you "press your luck?"

7. Where did we come up with the saying "it is none of your beeswax?"

8. Why does someone say "heads up" when you should be ducking?

9. Why do we say it was an "uphill battle?"

10. If something "goes without saying," why do we say it anyway?

11. If Australia is "down under" is the U.S. "up over" to the Australians?

12. Why do we say “down the hatch” when we don’t have a hatch?

13. Did Daniel Boone come up with saying “grin and bear it?”

14. If you are rolling dice or shooting craps, is it a “crap shoot?”

15. Why is it called “when Mother Nature calls” when it could be called “when Father Nature calls?”

16. Why do we say “we’ve been through this rodeo before” when we are not at a rodeo?

17. Can anything be “tough as nails” besides nails?

18. Why would you need to “scrape the bottom of the barrel?”

19. What “plate” do we step up to?

20. How does “whatever floats your boat” work?

21. If you cut objects, does that make you a “cut up?”

22. Do you provide “lip service?”

23. How do you “catch someone’s drift?”

24. Do you know anyone strong enough that “wild horses couldn’t drag them away?”

25. Why do we “cut someone off at the pass?”

26. How do we “catch someone on the flip side?”

27. Why do we need “wriggle room?”

28. If you are “down in the dumps” are you dumpster diving?

29. Are you playing a sport when you say, “no harm no foul?”

30. When you are in Rome, why do you do as the Romans do?

31. Where did the saying “going down to the wire” come from?

32. Have you ever got the “short end of the stick?”

33. How can you “hang on every word?”

34. How do you “get things going in the right direction?”

35. What "comes with the territory?"

36. If "something is too good to be true, it probably is" true?

37. Is the difference between men and boys, the size of their toys?

38. Why must all good things come to an end?

39. Where does the saying "hunky dory" come from?

40. Do desperate times really deserve desperate measures?

41. Did your left hand ever not know what your right hand was doing?

42. What is the "nature" of the beast?

43. Why do you "take a page" out of your own book?

44. When you "lose the handle," how do you find it?

45. When you "thread the needle," are you sewing or having a close encounter?

46. When we keep doing something over and over, why is it called "going right back to the well?"

47. Why would you "take the ball and run with it?"

SIGHT

1. Does everyone have a "mind's eye?"

2. How do you "peel your eyes" when you are told to "keep your eyes peeled?"

3. If you are "blind as a bat," do you use echolocation?

4. Is "seeing believing?"

5. Have you ever seen the "tip of the iceberg?"

6. Where do you buy an "eye opener?"

7. Does it mean that you now can see after being blind if you are "blind sighted?"

8. Are there "seeing eye" humans for blind dogs?

9. If you saw a blind person on a segue, would you move over?

10. If you are cross-eyed and have dyslexia, can you read all right?

11. If you eat a lot of carrots, can you see better?

12. Why doesn't a vampire have a reflection in a mirror?

13. How do you "catch" someone's eye?

14. How can something become a "sight for sore eyes?"

SIGNS

1. Why is it necessary to have a door where the sign reads "keep this door closed at all times?"

2. Why do road signs read "Keep Right" and "Merge Left" together?

3. Why do "Slow Children" warning signs have images of running children?

4. How would you not know something even if it "hit you upside your head?"

5. If sign makers went on strike, what do they put on their signs?

6. How do "Do not walk on the grass" signs get there?

7. When there are two doors, why is there usually a sign on one of them that reads "use other door?"

8. Can you have an "original reproduction?"

9. Why is it necessary to "read the writing on the wall?"

10. If you see a lookout sign should you lookout?

SLEEP

1. How do you “sleep tight?”

2. If people tell you that you will regret something in the morning, should you sleep until noon?

3. Who figured out “let sleeping dogs lie?”

4. Have you seen anyone “asleep at the wheel?”

5. Does it become better if you sleep on it?

6. When you go to bed, why is it called “hitting the sack?”

7. How do you “sleep like a dog?”

8. If a child refuses to sleep during nap time, are they guilty of “resisting a rest?”

9. Do you yawn in your sleep?

SPACE

1. How do we know that we aren't being watched by someone in the 4th dimension?

2. Which way is up and down in space?

3. Who discovered "what goes up must come down?"

4. If the "sky is the limit," then what is space?

5. How do you know something is "out of this world?"

6. Where do the limits of infinity end?

7. Do you need to be an astronaut to get "spaced out?"

8. How can something "come out of nowhere?"

9. Why is it called a "Moon Walk" when it is performed on Earth?

STUPIDITY

1. Who discovered that two dummies can out vote a genius?

2. If knowledge is power, is stupidity a weakness?

3. How does "stupid is as stupid does" work?

4. Could the problem with gene "pool" be that there is no lifeguard?

5. Are you depriving some village of its idiot?

6. If you would remove all of the warning labels, would that take care of all the stupid people?

7. If you think how stupid the "average" person is then do you realize half of them are stupider than that?

8. Why is there no law against stupidity?

9. How can someone be "dumb as a rock?"

10. Do you know how it feels not to be the "sharpest pencil in the box?"

11. Have you ever been told that "if idiots could fly, this location would be an airport?"

12. How does "falling off a turnip truck" cause stupidity?

13. If you make "stupid mistakes," can you make "smart mistakes?"

SUCCESS VS. FAILURE

1. Who stated, “Get comfortable with being wrong, it’s going to happen a lot?”

2. Why do we state, “that’s my story (excuse) and I am sticking to it?”

3. Why if you want something done right, do you have to do it yourself?

4. Have you realized that “if you’re not part of the solution, then you are part of the problem?”

5. Why is common sense like a deodorant, those who need it are the least likely to use it?

6. Do you know someone who has never been wrong, but has been mistaken a lot?

7. Is “change for the better” always better?

8. If quitters never win and winners never quit, who decided to “quit while you’re ahead?”

9. Why is it success always occurs in private and failure happens in full view of everyone?

10. Why do we say it was an “uphill battle” while others say, “it was all downhill from there?”

11. If "there is a will there is a way", if there is no will is there no way?

12. How can you be "out of gas" and "gassed" at the same time?

13. How do you become a "gluttons for punishment?

14. Why does a celebrity work hard to be successful and well-known, then wears glasses and tries to avoid being recognized?

15. What happens when you can't get a "handle on something?"

16. How do you "shower" praise on someone?

17. Why is it called "the icing on the cake" when we are finished with a project?

18. When you get nowhere, why is it called "hitting a brick wall?"

19. Why do you "touch base" with someone?

20. Are you an acrobat when you "jump through hoops?"

21. Why is something either "feast or famine?"

22. When you don't want to do something, why are "your hands tied?"

23. Should you float downstream when you get "up a creek without a paddle?"

24. What do you do when you are "put in pinch?"

25. What happens when you "play your cards right?"

26. Why do you "chase your tail?"

27. How do you "level the playing field?"

28. If something "cracks you up," can it be repaired?

29. If you "give someone a hand," which hand do you give them?

30. What happens when you get to the "top of the heap?"

31. When you "wrap it up," what are you wrapping?

32. Where are you when you are "on easy street?"

33. When you make a "clean sweep," what is swept clean?

34. Why would you give someone "a leg up?"

35. When you are told to "dig deeper," what are you digging for?

36. Why "if there is no pain, is there no gain?"

37. How do you "take the world by storm?"

38. When someone "eats your lunch," why are you not talking about food?

39. How many holes have you "dug yourself out of?

40. Have you ever had "the wheels come off?"

41. Instead of "sweating the small stuff," do you "pet the sweaty stuff?"

42. Why do you need to know "which side your bread is buttered on?"

43. Why would you "leave no stone unturned?"

44. When you “nail it down,” what are you nailing?

45. Does it hurt to be on “pins and needles?”

46. How does a person make themselves if they are “self-made?”

47. Have you ever played for “all the marbles?”

48. How do you ‘put it all on the line?”

49. Is sarcasm really for “winners?”

50. When you “take one for the team,” what are you taking?

51. Why was the “Great Escape” great?

52. At the end of the day, why doesn’t it matter?

53. How do you determine the “lay of the land?”

54. How do you get “the world at your feet?”

55. Why would you want to “work like a dog?”

56. How do you “get it together?”

57. Do you really climb a ladder when "climbing the ladder of success?"

58. If you are "outstanding in your field, are you standing in a pasture?

59. Do things turn out best for the people that do the best for the way things turn out?

60. How do you know something is your "cup of tea?"

61. How can you tell something is "not in the cards," especially if you're not playing cards?

62. How can you tell when "opportunity knocks?"

63. When you don't meet expectations and don't succeed, why are you said to have "laid an egg?"

64. What rock do you hit when you reach "rock bottom?"

65. How do you "make your mark?"

66. If you find something you are looking for in the last place you look, why didn't you look there first?

67. How do you “work your tail off,” especially if you don’t have a tail?

68. Does being “slow on the trigger” only matter if you are in a duel?

69. How can something “take the wind out of your sail” when you don’t have a boat?

TIME

1. Why must “all good things come to an end?”

2. Did you know a broken clock is still right twice a day?

3. When “good things happen to those who wait,” do “bad things happen to those who don’t wait?”

4. Why is there “no time like the present?”

5. How do you “spend quality time” and how do you earn it?

6. If you want time to fly, do you just throw your watch out the window?

7. If “time flies,” where does it go to?

8. Is it okay to use AM radio in the afternoon?

9. Is there a time limit on fortune cookie predictions?

10. “A stich in time saves nine” what?

11. If you are part of a neighborhood “watch,” are you required to give people the correct time?

12. Why is Monday so far from Friday, and Friday so close to Monday?

13. Is your "alone time" for everyone's safety?

14. What is a "nick of time?"

15. Why would you "hurry up and wait?"

16. When waiting, why are you told to "hang tight?"

17. How do you "get your clock cleaned?"

18. Why would you "make a long story short?"

19. Why does something happen only "once in a blue moon?"

20. How do you "make up for lost time?"

21. If you have "time to spare," can you save it for later?

22. Why is it "better to be late than never" to get somewhere?

23. Why is a "detailed summary" necessary?

24. Is it really the last minute, when we wait "to the last minute?"

25. Can something that is expedited be expedited?

26. How do you "take time out" of the day?

27. Is an old clock a reminder of time past?

28. How do you "stand the test of time?"

WEATHER

1. Why when it is raining and there is lightning and thunder, it starts to rain harder?

2. Have you ever seen a "cloud with a silver lining?"

3. How do you "skate on thin ice?"

4. If hot air rises, what keeps some people on the ground?

5. How can someone be "walking on air?"

6. Why does it "rain on your parade?"

7. What kind of weather is "not fit for a dog?"

8. If you are "in a fog," is it due to the weather?

9. When you "don't have the foggiest idea," do you wait for the weather to clear?

10. How can something be "right as rain?"

11. When you lick the air does it get wet?

12. Have you ever seen it rain cats and dogs?

13. Why do we "make hay while the sun shines?

14. Have you ever seen rain come down in buckets?

15. Are you really talking about wind when you talk about "taking the wind out of your sails?"

16. How do you find "any port in a storm" when you are on land?

17. How do you "catch lightning" in a bottle?

18. What is the "crack" of dawn?

19. How do you "steal someone's thunder?"

20. How do you get "under the weather?"

21. How do you "shoot the breeze?"

22. How can a storm be "hairy?"

23. If a storm can be "bad," can there be a "good" storm?

24. How can your "tail feathers get wet," when you don't have feathers or a tail?

WHO?

1. If "people in glass houses shouldn't throw stones", should people in stone houses not throw glass?

2. Who discovered that a chain is "only as strong as its weakest link?"

3. Who figured out Rome wasn't built in a day?

4. Who determined "if you build it they will come?"

5. Who found out "Elvis has left the building?"

6. Who figured out "if the shoe fits wear it?"

7. Who swims in a "motor pool?"

WOMEN

1. Why are both the footwear and the underwear of women called "thongs?"

2. Why can you still move your lips when you apply lipstick?

3. Why don't you find out what happiness is until you get married?

4. If a man speaks in a forest and there is no woman to hear him, is he still wrong?

5. Are women seeking to be equal to men lacking ambition?

6. Why can't women put on mascara with their mouths closed?

7. Why do we choose from two people for President and 50 women for Miss America?

8. If a woman says "what" to what you said, is it possibly to give you a second chance to change your mind?

9. How do you become "giddy as a schoolgirl?"

10. Is the quickest way for a woman to get something, is to make her husband think it's his idea?

11. Do all women "shop until they drop?"

Steve Vogt was born on January 22, 1950 in Wood River, Illinois. Vogt graduated from Civic Memorial High School in Bethalto, Illinois in 1968. During that time he went through both the Boy Scouts and Explorer Scouts. He was awarded the Eagle Scout Rank in 1966, having 60 merits badges. Vogt then graduated from Southern Illinois University in 1972 with a Bachelor of Science Degree. He had two children, Amber and Brock, and started teaching middle school science for the Maries County R-2 School District in 1974. Vogt retired in 2003 after 29 years of teaching and driving a school bus route. He was voted "Teacher of the Year" twice. He also served as Mayor and Alderman in his community for a total of 30 years.

Vogt served (and still serving) on various boards and committees. These include the Meramec Regional Planning Commission as the Operations Committee Chairman, Secretary, Treasurer, and Vice Chairman; the Belle Community Betterment Association; Meramec Regional Community Foundation (local and regional boards); Belle High School Washington D.C. Trip sponsor; the Belle Volunteer Fire Department as Second Lieutenant and Assistant Chief; Maries County Extension Council; Enterprize Zone Board; Meramec Regional Solid Waste Executive Board as Secretary and Treasurer; Transportation Advisory Committee; the Vienna Eagles Club; Lions Club; the Belle Chamber of Commerce; the Belle Fair Board; Friends of the Belle Library; MSTA President; and still drives trips for local sports teams and substitute teaches.

This project was made possible, in part, by generous support from the Osage Arts Community.

Osage Arts Community provides temporary time, space and support for the creation of new artistic works in a retreat format, serving creative people of all kinds — visual artists, composers, poets, fiction and nonfiction writers. Located on a 152-acre farm in an isolated rural mountainside setting in Central Missouri and bordered by ¾ of a mile of the Gasconade River, OAC provides residencies to those working alone, as well as welcoming collaborative teams, offering living space and workspace in a country environment to emerging and mid-career artists. For more information, visit us at www.osageac.org

Osage Arts Community

www.ingramcontent.com/pod-product-compliance
Lightning Source LLC
Chambersburg PA
CBHW030326100526
44592CB00010B/579
9781950380527